Write
Haiku

Lisa Holewa

Publishing Credits

Rachelle Cracchiolo, M.S.Ed., *Publisher*
Conni Medina, M.A.Ed., *Managing Editor*
Nika Fabienke, Ed.D., *Series Developer*
June Kikuchi, *Content Director*
Michelle Jovin, M.A., *Assistant Editor*
Lee Aucoin, *Senior Graphic Designer*

TIME For Kids and the TIME For Kids logo are registered trademarks of TIME Inc. Used under license.

Image Credits: p.5 Photos 12/Alamy Stock Photo; p.13 Heritage Image Partnership Ltd/Alamy Stock Photo; all other images from iStock and/or Shutterstock.

Teacher Created Materials
5301 Oceanus Drive
Huntington Beach, CA 92649-1030
http://www.tcmpub.com
ISBN 978-1-4258-4963-4
© 2018 Teacher Created Materials, Inc.

Table of Contents

All Around Us

Have you ever looked closely at a pinecone, a leaf, or a flower? If you have, you might have seen **patterns**.

There are patterns in nature. Patterns can show us how things are made. Patterns also help us make new things. Writers use patterns, too. Haiku (hi-KOO) are an example of this. They are poems based on patterns. They are usually about nature.

Began in Japan

The art from of haiku is over 800 years old. It came from Japan. But it was not popular right away. It took hundreds of years for it to catch on. Haiku masters like Matsuo Bashō (mah-TSOO-oh bah-SHO) helped it grow.

Patterns

To find patterns, you must look closely. Start by asking questions. Can I see how this is made? Do I see the same parts again and again? If the answers to these questions are yes, you may have found a pattern.

Plants and seashells have patterns. Trees and butterfly wings have them, too. The patterns may form triangles. Or they may spiral out from the center.

This shell spirals out from the center to make room for the growing animal inside.

Patterns in Writing

Writers and poets use patterns, too. Poets may repeat words or sounds at the end of each line. Writers may make all of their sentences the same length. Sometimes, a poem's **structure** can send a message.

These patterns can give words more power. Haiku is based on patterns. They help poets tell strong stories.

Play Day

maggie and milly and molly and may
went down to the beach (to play one day)

—E. E. Cummings

Look at the names in the first line of this poem. They are all lowercase, and they all start with the same letter. Do you think the girls might be the same in other ways?

Haiku Dos and Don'ts

Haiku does not have any rules. But there are some **traits** that most haiku poems share.

Do Give a Nod to Nature

Most haiku poems describe scenes in nature. They may tell a tale about animals. Or, they may make the reader think of a time of year. Flowers may make the reader think of spring. Fireflies may be used to describe a warm summer night.

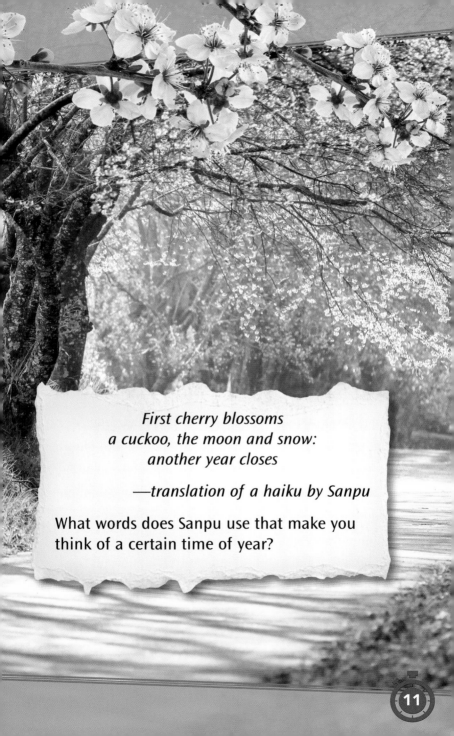

First cherry blossoms
a cuckoo, the moon and snow:
another year closes

—*translation of a haiku by Sanpu*

What words does Sanpu use that make you think of a certain time of year?

Do Write Three Lines

Most English haiku are three lines long. Each line follows a pattern with sounds. These sounds are called **syllables**. Haiku usually have 17 syllables. The lines follow this pattern:

The first line has five.
The second line has seven.
The third line has five.

Did you notice that was a haiku?

bird	lion	elephant
1 syllable	2 syllables	3 syllables

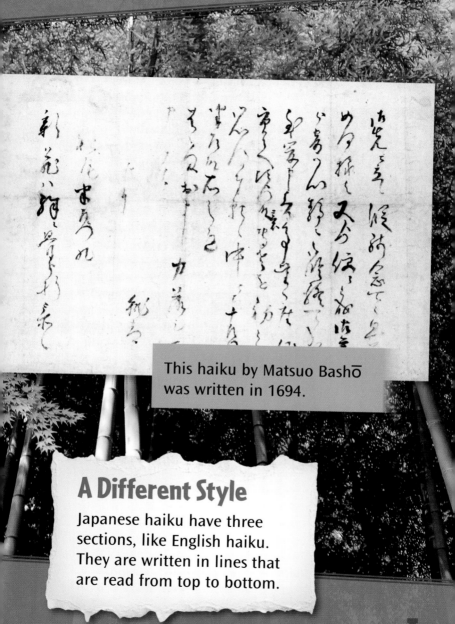

This haiku by Matsuo Bashō was written in 1694.

A Different Style

Japanese haiku have three sections, like English haiku. They are written in lines that are read from top to bottom.

Most haiku poets follow the same patterns. There are also traits that most poets try to avoid.

Don't Just Say It

Haiku poets try not to just say what they are feeling. Instead, they describe a scene. This makes the reader feel a certain way. Most haiku poets would not write "I felt so lonely." Instead, they would write about a frog alone in a still pond.

Don't Make It Too Long

Most English haiku have 17 syllables. Japanese haiku always have 17 *ons*. An *on* is a sound that forms words. English haiku poets try to follow the same pattern with syllables. But they do not have to do this.

In fact, there is only one rule for the length of haiku poems. A reader should be able to say the whole poem in one breath. So do not make it too long!

Make sure readers can say your
haiku without losing their breath!

17

Do-It-Yourself

Now that you know the patterns of haiku, you can try writing your own.

Step 1: Look Outside

If you are near a window, look outside. What do you see? If you cannot see nature right now, think. Did you notice something the last time you were outside? Maybe you saw leaves blowing in the wind. Or, maybe you saw a squirrel running up a tree. Try to capture the scene in your haiku.

From the Desk Of...

You can write haiku without being in nature. Just imagine what you might see. These poems are called *desk haiku*. They are not written from an actual moment but from an imagined or remembered one.

Step 2: Write It All Down

After you have picked a scene you want to share with the reader, start by writing a sentence. Describe what you saw. Try to make the reader see the same thing.

Do not worry if it does not look like a haiku yet. Just get your thoughts down on paper.

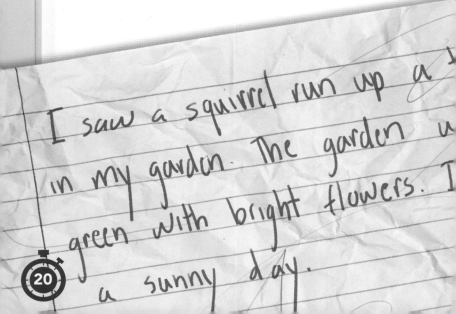

I saw a squirrel run up a in my garden. The garden u green with bright flowers. I a sunny day.

Step 3: Rearrange

Now that you have written about your image, you can make it into a haiku. Try splitting it into three lines. You might need to add or change a thought.

Next, count the syllables in each line. Can you make your idea fit in 17 syllables? If not, do not worry! Just make sure the reader can say it in a single breath.

Step 4: Share Your Scene

After you are done, share your haiku with friends and family. Ask if they feel the same thing you felt when you wrote the poem. If not, go back and **revise** your work. When you are done, write your haiku on a new sheet of paper. Then, display your work!

National Haiku Writing Month

Write one haiku each day in February. That is when National Haiku Writing Month takes place. The event started in the United States. But it has spread all over the world.

My Haiku

Bright sun and cool breeze
Squirrels run up and down trees
Garden flowers sway

25

Picking Out Patterns

As you have read, patterns are all around us. They are in nature and in writing. Poets use them to make their writing more powerful.

You can find and use patterns, too. Read some haiku. See if you can spot any patterns. Then, try to add some to your writing. Pretty soon, you will be a pattern pro!

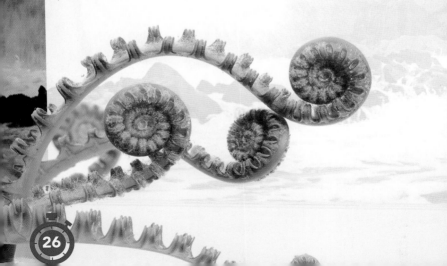

Winner!

The World Children's Haiku Contest takes place every two years. Children can send in their own drawings and haiku. The winners get prizes. They also get published in a book.

Glossary

patterns—things that are repeated

revise—to make changes to correct and improve something

structure—the way something is built or organized

syllables—the parts that words are split into when they are said out loud

traits—things that make people or things different from others